My Name Starts With S

By Larry Hayes

To Stan, to my sisters, Rita and Lana, and to my sons, Jeffrey, Rob, Devon, Gabriel, & Nathanael— all shining stars in my life—I dedicate this book of S.

Featuring the art of
Airlie Anderson

A   B   C   D   E
F   G   H   I   J
K   L   M   N   O
P   Q   R   S   T
U   V   W   X   Y   Z

ISBN 0-9725292-1-7

c

My name
starts with S.
I spell it

S _____

Mommy and Daddy
say
my name is special.

Place
photo
of child
here

Just like me!

C

Some s's are small and
some S's are big.
See the animals starting
with big S.

Seahorse

Shark

Steer

Skunk

Sea lion

Sheep

Squirrel

Salamander

Sloth

Spoonbill

Big **S** is the letter
that begins the
names of these
four friends:

Sarah

Stan

Steve

Sally

9

Things that I see begin with small s.

stilts

shell

statue

silver siren

school

Three silly sons
sporting
sweaters,
sandals,
and socks
on stone steps

snake
skeleton

shoe

scarf

stamp

sunflower

shield

steeple

sunglasses

snow

ship at sunset

stripes and spots

stadium

scoreboard

street sweeper

Count the S's
you see here.

Slipping and sliding
on a slippery slope
on Saturdays
and Sundays is
spectacular
and scary!

15

I savor foods that start with s.

sugar & spice

strawberry

salad

sliced salami

sausages

strudel

shakes & smoothies

spaghetti with
sauce

The sky and space are full of words with S.

star cluster

space station

solar system

stunt plane

Saturn

s   c boom s   s

s   l
galaxy

stars

sun

space shuttle

19

I see things at the seashore that start with s.

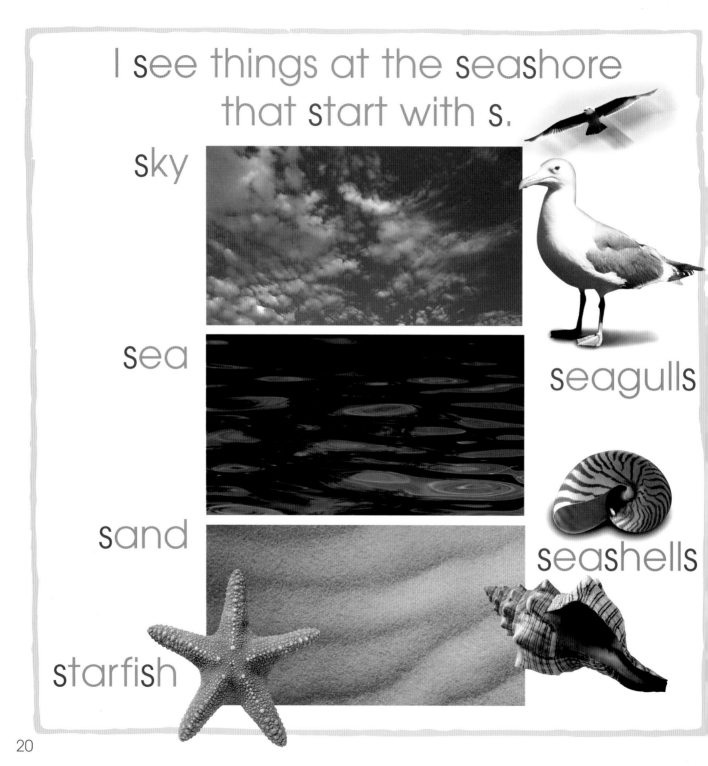

sky

sea

seagulls

sand

seashells

starfish

Touch the S's and trace their shape.

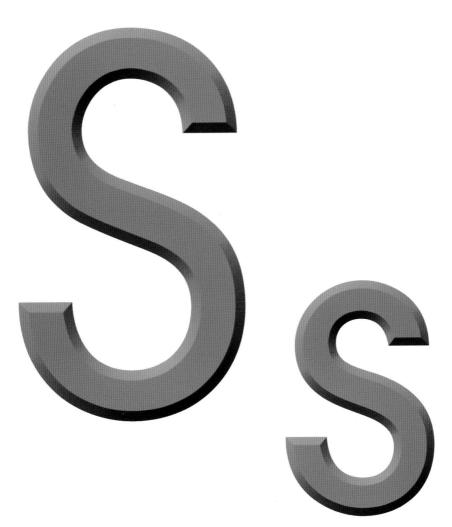

Can you find the things starting with **S** on the next page?

There are sensational places in the world starting with S.

Seattle

Sacramento

Salem

San Francisco

San Diego

Scottsdale

Salt Lake City

Santa Fe

San Antonio

South Dakota

Saint Paul

Springfield

Lake Superior

Syracus[e]

South Carolina

Saint Augustin[e]

Savannah

Saint Louis

Saint Petersburg

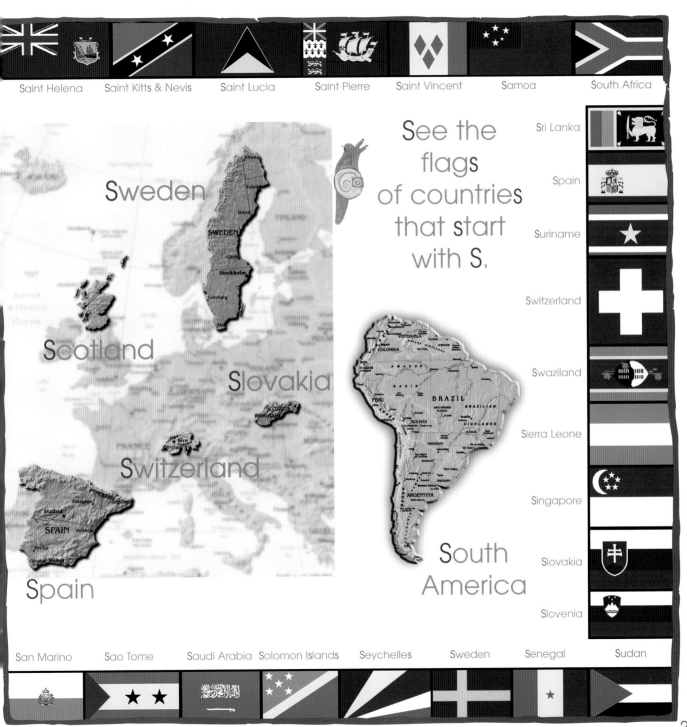

Saint Helena | Saint Kitts & Nevis | Saint Lucia | Saint Pierre | Saint Vincent | Samoa | South Africa

See the
flags
of countries
that start
with S.

Sweden

Scotland

Slovakia

Switzerland

Spain

South
America

Sri Lanka

Spain

Suriname

Switzerland

Swaziland

Sierra Leone

Singapore

Slovakia

Slovenia

San Marino | Sao Tome | Saudi Arabia | Solomon Islands | Seychelles | Sweden | Senegal | Sudan

Even things we do
start with S.

Swinging

Stretching

Stomping
and splashing

Singing songs

Somersaulting

Skiing

Strolling and strumming

Sleeping side by side

Sitting

Sharing snacks

Mommy and Daddy
are right.
My name is
special!

It starts with

How many snails did you see in this book?

Did you find these S objects on page 23?

sky	shrimp
sea	seal
stars	smile
shooting star	swimming mermaid
Saturn	submarine
swans	snail
sneakers	shark
squirrel snorkeling	saddle

Most importantly, did you have fun reading?

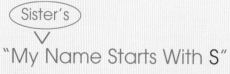

In an emergency dial 911 and help will be sent.

(A public service page)

My Name Starts With

Larry Hayes, Inspire Publications SAN: 2 5 5 -1 2 2 5
13229 Middle Canyon Road
Carmel Valley, CA 93924
831-917-6059 or toll free: 877-820-1473

Illustrations by Airlie Anderson
Book Design by Jenny Q. Sandrof of Blue Heron Design Group

Credits
Solar System Illustration Credit, p.18: Greg Bacon (STScI), NASA.
Sonic Boom p.19: USN; other space & shuttle photos: NASA
Other photos by Larry Hayes

Find us on the World Wide Web at
www.MyNameStartsWith.com
My Name Starts With is a registered trademark
of Larry Hayes

ISBN 0-9725292-1-7

Sleep tight with
sweet dreams
tonight!